COMPARISONS

OF

PARLIAMENTARY AUTHORITIES

Self-study quizzes to compare and contrast

American Institute of Parliamentarians
Standard Code of Parliamentary Procedures

Robert's Rules of Order Newly Revised, 11th edition

Demeter's Manual of Parliamentary Law and Procedure

Riddick's Rules of Procedure

American Institute of Parliamentarians
Education Department
2013

© 2013
By American Institute of Parliamentarians
(888) 664-0428
www.aipparl.org
aip@aipparl.org

Produced in the United States of America.

ISBN: 978-0-942736-31-1
Printed July 2015
2 3 4 5 6 7 8 9 10

Produced by the
2013 Education Department
American Institute of Parliamentarians
Jeanette N. Williams, CP-T, Education Director
Ruth S. Ryan, CP-T, Assistant Education Director
Ann Rempel, CPP-T, Printed Materials Division Chair
Alison Wallis, CP-T, President
with assistance from
Linda Juteau, CPP-T

TABLE OF CONTENTS

This page intentionally left blank.

INTRODUCTION

Comparisons of Parliamentary Authorities is based on the 1996 book *The Point is … Do you Know the Answer*, which was compiled by the late Miriam Butcher, CPP-T, a former president of AIP. While inspired by that book, the first edition of *Comparisons* (2009) went well beyond being a mere update. Most of the questions were rewritten, and sections of the original book were reorganized. New sections on each specific class of motions, documents of authority, order of business, boards and committees, electronic meetings, methods of voting, and disciplinary action were added.

The second edition has been updated with references to the 11th edition of *Robert's Rules of Order Newly Revised* (RONR) and *American Institute of Parliamentarians Standard Code of Parliamentary Procedure* (AIPSC). New material on electronic voting has been added.

Comparisons is designed to broaden readers' parliamentary knowledge and to challenge students in their use of parliamentary research.

ACKNOWLEDGEMENTS

The AIP Education Department is grateful to Jonathan Jacobs, CPP, for researching and updating the questions and answers for the first edition of *Comparisons*. Special thanks go to Ruth Ryan, CP-T; Linda Juteau, CPP-T; and Teresa Stone, CP, for their work in updating the questions and answers for the second edition in 2013.

In addition, the department is very appreciative of the work of Kay Allison Crews, CP, who formats publications for the AIP Education Department.

ABBREVIATIONS

Dem   *Demeter's Manual of Parliamentary Law and Procedure,* © 1969

RIDDICK   *Riddick's Rules of Procedure,* © 1985

RONR   *Robert's Rules of Order Newly Revised,* 11th Edition, © 2011

AIPSC   *American Institute of Parliamentarians Standard Code of Parliamentary Procedure* © 2012

T   RONR Tinted pages

Note: The answers indicated may be only some of the possible responses to the question posed. You may further challenge yourself by reviewing all references to the topic on your own.

QUESTIONS

CHAPTERS 1 –12

This page intentionally left blank.

CHAPTER 1 Member Rights

QUESTION	DEM	RIDDICK	RONR	AIPSC
1. What are the fundamental rights of a member?				
2. Who is considered to be a member in good standing?				
3. What is meant by *honorary membership*?				
4. Does an absent member have any rights?				
5. Are members' rights ever suspended?				
6. How does a member exercise his or her right to have the rules enforced?				
7. What are a member's voting rights?				
8. How may membership rights be terminated?				

QUESTION	DEM	RIDDICK	RONR	AIPSC
9. When does a resignation become effective?				
10. Does a member have a right to ask a question during a business meeting?				
11. What can a member do in a meeting if he or she does not know what procedure or motion would be in order?				
12. May an organization assess fees aside from dues?				
13. What rights does a member lose when his or her dues are unpaid?				
14. Does a member have a right to inspect the minutes of the organization?				

Comparisons

CHAPTER 2 Subsidiary Motions

	QUESTION	DEM	RIDDICK	RONR	AIPSC
1.	How can members "kill" a main motion without a direct vote on the motion?				
2.	Which motion is used to change the text of a pending motion?				
3.	What are the different forms of the subsidiary motion to *Amend*?				
4.	What is meant by an amendment being *germane*?				
5.	Can amendments be hostile to the pending question?				
6.	What is meant by *friendly amendment*?				
7.	What is meant by a *substitute amendment*?				
8.	Can motions that rank higher in precedence than the motion to *Amend* be amended?				

QUESTION	DEM	RIDDICK	RONR	AIPSC
9. How can members deal with unlimited suggestions for a particular choice in a pending question?				
10. How can the assembly send a motion to a committee?				
11. What is the difference between a standing and a special committee?				
12. How is a special committee formed?				
13. How can a member delay consideration of a motion for a specific period of time?				
14. How long can the assembly postpone consideration of a pending question?				
15. How is a special order created?				
16. What are the general limits of debate?				
17. How are the limits of debate set?				

Comparisons

QUESTION	DEM	RIDDICK	RONR	AIPSC
18. How can members stop debate?				
19. How long can a question be laid on the table?				
20. What vote is required to adopt the subsidiary motion to Amend?				
21. Does "question" called from the floor require the chair to close debate?				

This page intentionally left blank.

Comparisons

CHAPTER 3
Privileged Motions

QUESTION	DEM	RIDDICK	RONR	AIPSC
1. Why can privileged motions always be made when a main motion is pending?				
2. Which privileged motions can sometimes interrupt a speaker?				
3. What is meant by the term *Call for the Orders of the Day*?				
4. If someone calls for the orders of the day, how can the assembly decide to set aside the agenda or to continue with the pending question?				
5. What is a question of privilege affecting the assembly?				
6. What is a question of personal privilege?				
7. What can members do if they disagree with the ruling of the chair on admissibility of a question of privilege?				

QUESTION	DEM	RIDDICK	RONR	AIPSC
8. How can the assembly take a "short break" in the meeting?				
9. How does a meeting *stand at ease*?				
10. How do members terminate a meeting?				
11. What motion is used to continue a meeting several days away?				
12. Which privileged motions can be raised as main motions?				
13. Which privileged motions cannot be amended?				

CHAPTER 4
Incidental Motions

	QUESTION	DEM	RIDDICK	RONR	AIPSC
1.	When can a point of order be raised? Are there any exceptions?				
2.	What decisions of the chair cannot be appealed?				
3.	Under what conditions is an appeal debatable?				
4.	What is the usual vote required for suspension of the rules?				
5.	Can all rules be suspended?				
6.	What are the conditions under which the bylaws can be suspended?				
7.	What is meant by the "Gordian Knot" motion?				
8.	How can a motion be separated into two or more parts? Does this apply only to main motions?				

QUESTION	DEM	RIDDICK	RONR	AIPSC
9. When can a motion be divided upon demand?				
10. What is the method for verifying a voice vote?				
11. What is the method for having a vote counted?				
12. How can an assembly take a ballot vote?				
13. What is the vote required to close nominations? Why is it higher than the vote to re-open nominations?				
14. What are the methods for making nominations?				
15. What is the procedure used for resigning?				
16. Does a member need permission to read from correspondence or a book while speaking in debate?				
17. Is asking a speaker a question permitted?				

QUESTION	DEM	RIDDICK	RONR	AIPSC
18. How can a member find out which motion to make or if something is in order?				
19. How is a request for an unspecified privilege handled?				
20. Does the motion *Object to the Consideration of a Question* affect members' rights?				
21. How does the chair put the vote on an *Objection to the Consideration of a Question*?				

This page intentionally left blank.

CHAPTER 5
Motions That Bring the Question Back

	QUESTION	DEM	RIDDICK	RONR	AIPSC
1.	After a motion is sent to a committee, how can the assembly resume consideration of the motion?				
2.	What happens to a standing committee when the motion is returned to the assembly?				
3.	What happens to a special committee when a motion is returned to the assembly?				
4.	What vote is needed to reconsider the vote on a main motion?				
5.	When is it impossible to reconsider a main motion?				
6.	Can a vote on a subsidiary motion be reconsidered?				
7.	What is the time limit involved in reconsidering a motion?				

QUESTION	DEM	RIDDICK	RONR	AIPSC
8. What is the motion to *Reconsider and Enter* on the minutes?"				
9. When can a motion to *Rescind* a motion not be used?				
10. What motion is used to change the text of a previously adopted motion?				
11. What is meant by the motion to *Rescind and Expunge*?" What vote is required and how does this affect the previously approved minutes?				
12. By what process may a defeated motion be restored to consideration?				
13. What vote is required to amend bylaws?				

CHAPTER 6
Meeting and Quorum

	QUESTION	DEM	RIDDICK	RONR	AIPSC
1.	What kinds of meetings are there?				
2.	What is an annual meeting?				
3.	What is the difference between a meeting and a session?				
4.	Does the time between regular meetings have any procedural effect?				
5.	What is an adjourned or a continued meeting?				
6.	What are the limits on special meetings?				
7.	Can an item rejected at one meeting be considered at another meeting?				

QUESTION	DEM	RIDDICK	RONR	AIPSC
8. What is an executive or closed session?				
9. How are the minutes of an executive session handled?				
10. What is a quorum?				
11. How is a quorum calculated?				
12. What actions can be taken in the absence of a quorum?				
13. How can an action that is taken at a meeting without a quorum be made legitimate?				
14. What is a "point of no quorum?"				
15. What rules apply to electronic meetings?				
16. May committees meet electronically?				

Comparisons

CHAPTER 7
Order of Business and Debate

	QUESTION	DEM	RIDDICK	RONR	AIPSC
1.	What is the standard order of business?				
2.	What is an agenda and how does it become effective?				
3.	What is a consent agenda or a consent calendar?				
4.	Is there a difference between an agenda and a program?				
5.	How can members change the order of business?				
6.	How can the assembly take up something that is scheduled later in the order of business?				
7.	Can a member give his right to debate to another member?				

QUESTION	DEM	RIDDICK	RONR	AIPSC
8. What is considered improper debate?				
9. How can a non-member enter into debate?				
10. Under what circumstances can the presiding officer enter into debate?				
11. What actions can be taken when a member enters into improper debate?				
12. What are the rules for assigning the floor?				

CHAPTER 8
Voting

	QUESTION	DEM	RIDDICK	RONR	AIPSC
1.	How is a majority determined?				
2.	When is the president entitled to vote?				
3.	May honorary members vote?				
4.	What is a two-thirds vote?				
5.	What is meant by a vote of a majority of the membership?				
6.	What is a plurality voting?				
7.	What is meant by a cumulative vote?				
8.	What is a straw vote?				

QUESTION	DEM	RIDDICK	RONR	AIPSC
9. What is the function of proxy voting?				
10. What are the methods of voting?				
11. How can someone be elected who was not nominated?				
12. How are the results of a voice vote verified?				
13. Are illegal votes counted in determining a majority?				
14. May ex officio members vote?				
15. Can a member abstain?				
16. When can a member change his or her vote?				
17. What is preferential voting?				

QUESTION	DEM	RIDDICK	RONR	AIPSC
18. What is ballot voting?				
19. How is a roll call vote conducted?				
20. How can an election be conducted when there is only one nominee for an office?				
21. When should a mail ballot be used?				
22. Is a vote valid if the motion was not seconded?				
23. What is bullet voting?				
24. What is absentee voting?				
25. What are voting cards?				
26. What is electronic voting?				

QUESTION	DEM	RIDDICK	RONR	AIPSC
27. What is a signed ballot?				
28. How long should ballots be kept?				
29. What is the principle of one person-one vote?				

CHAPTER 9
Officers and Documents of Authority

QUESTION	DEM	RIDDICK	RONR	AIPSC
1. What defines the offices and the duties of the officers of an organization?				
2. What is the minimum number of officers necessary for conducting business?				
3. What are the procedural duties of the presiding officer?				
4. How are vacancies filled? What about vacancies in the office of president?				
5. Who presides if the president and vice president are absent from the meeting?				
6. Does the president have the power to appoint committees?				
7. How should the presiding officer be referred to by the members and by himself?				

QUESTION	DEM	RIDDICK	RONR	AIPSC
8. What items go into the minutes?				
9. How are minutes approved when there is only one meeting per year?				
10. Minutes have been approved and later an error is discovered. How may the minutes be corrected?				
11. Members cannot agree on the corrections to the minutes being approved. What do we do?				
12. A member wants to "dispense with the minutes." What does that mean?				
13. How is the treasurer's report verified?				
14. If the society has a separate constitution and bylaws, which is superior to the other?				
15. Does custom supersede the rules in a parliamentary manual?				
16. What is the vote needed for a society to adopt parliamentary rules that differ from the parliamentary authority?				

QUESTION	DEM	RIDDICK	RONR	AIPSC
17. Can a rule in the bylaws be suspended?				
18. What normally should be included in the bylaws?				
19. When do the rules in the parliamentary authority not apply?				

This page intentionally left blank.

CHAPTER 10
Boards and Committees

	QUESTION	DEM	RIDDICK	RONR	AIPSC
1.	Do all organizations have a board of directors?				
2.	Are officers automatically on the board of directors?				
3.	How is board procedure different from regular meeting procedure?				
4.	Can boards adopt their own rules?				
5.	I'm a member of the organization but not of the board. Can I attend board meetings?				
6.	How is an executive committee created?				
7.	How are standing committees created?				

QUESTION	DEM	RIDDICK	RONR	AIPSC
8. How are special committees created?				
9. What happens to an unfinished assignment to a special committee when a new administration is elected?				
10. Can people who are members of the organization, but not on the committee, attend committee meetings?				
11. What is done at a committee hearing?				
12. Can the chairman of a committee participate in debate in a committee meeting?				
13. Can committees appoint sub-committees?				
14. Are minority reports from committees automatically presented to the assembly?				
15. What can the assembly do if a committee doesn't report?				
16. What rules govern the reconsideration of a vote in a committee?				

Comparisons

CHAPTER 11
Disciplinary Actions

QUESTION	DEM	RIDDICK	RONR	AIPSC
1. How is an assembly protected from annoyance by nonmembers in a meeting?				
2. How does the chair deal with minor breaches of order by a member?				
3. What is "naming" a member?				
4. What are the rights of a member who is subjected to disciplinary procedures?				
5. How are offences that occur outside a meeting handled?				
6. Why shouldn't disciplinary actions take place in open session?				
7. Who can represent the accused in a trial?				

Comparisons

QUESTION	DEM	RIDDICK	RONR	AIPSC
8. How are officers removed under disciplinary procedures?				
9. What is a motion of censure and what effect does it have?				
10. What is a vote of no confidence and what effect does it have?				
11. What is "putting a motion from the member's place?"				
12. What are the grounds for expelling a member?				

CHAPTER 12
What is the Difference in the Terms?

TERMS	DEM	RIDDICK	RONR	AIPSC
1. Constitution – Bylaws				
2. Merger – Consolidation				
3. Precedence – Precedent				
4. Bylaws – Standing Rules				
5. Order of Business – Agenda				
6. Executive Board – Executive Committee				
7. Executive Board – Executive Session				

TERMS	DEM	RIDDICK	RONR	AIPSC
8. Candidate – Nominee				
9. Consensus – General/Unanimous Consent				
10. Recess – Adjourn –Stand at Ease				
11. Reconsider – Rescind				
12. Meeting – Session				
13. Privileged Motion – Question of Privilege				

Comparisons

ANSWERS

CHAPTERS 1 – 12

Note: The answers indicated may be only some of the possible responses to the question posed. You may further challenge yourself by reviewing all references to the topic on your own.

This page intentionally left blank.

CHAPTER 1
Member Rights

	QUESTION	DEM	RIDDICK	RONR	AIPSC
1.	What are the fundamental rights of a member?	20, 305	110-11	3, 263-64, 407-08	259-63, 265
2.	Who is considered to be a member in good standing?	306		6n	261
3.	What is meant by *honorary membership*?	304	99-100	463-64	181
4.	Does an absent member have any rights?	305	1	2, 4, 251, 263-64, 566, 595	111
5.	Are members' rights ever suspended?	208-09	208	406, 571-72, 660, 662	263-65
6.	How does a member exercise his or her right to have the rules enforced?	121	140-41	70, 247, 249-51	90-93
7.	What are a member's voting rights?	37-38	198	406-07	147, 157
8.	How may membership rights be terminated?	204, 266-67	174, 193	291-92, 667-68	263-65
9.	When does a resignation become effective?	205-07	110, 174	291-92	265-66
10.	Does a member have a right to ask a question during a business meeting?	90-93, 125-26	138-40	72, 292, 294-95	9-10
11.	What can a member do in a meeting if he or she does not know what procedure or motion would be in order?	124	138-40	72, 292, 293-94	93-96
12.	May an organization assess fees aside from dues?	20		572	259
13.	What rights does a member lose when his or her dues are unpaid?	239, 243, 306	198	406	261

QUESTION	DEM	RIDDICK	RONR	AIPSC
14. Does a member have a right to inspect the minutes of the organization?	23	111, 113	459, 460	260

CHAPTER 2
Subsidiary Motions

	QUESTION	DEM	RIDDICK	RONR	AIPSC
1.	How can members "kill" a main motion without a direct vote on the motion?	28, 66, 141	143-44, 158-59, 188, 189	63, 70, 126, 267-70	70-72
2.	Which motion is used to change the text of a pending motion?	68	12	63, 130, 296	50
3.	What are the different forms of the subsidiary motion to *Amend*?	76-79	13-15	133-35	50-51
4.	What is meant by an amendment being *germane*?	70-71, 81	97	131, 136-38	52-53
5.	Can amendments be hostile to the pending question?	72-73, 82		137	53
6.	What is meant by *friendly amendment*?		12-13	162	56, 274
7.	What is meant by a *substitute amendment*?	77, 79-82	13-14	115, 134, 153-56	54-55
8.	Can motions that rank higher in precedence than the motion to *Amend* be amended?	46-47, 62, 102	117	65, 132	58
9.	How can members deal with unlimited suggestions for a particular choice in a pending question?	146-47	70	162-67	55-56
10.	How can the assembly send a motion to a committee?	82	46-48	115, 168	58-59
11.	What is the difference between a standing and a special committee?	277	48-49	490-92	188-89
12.	How is a special committee formed?	84	49-50	171-72, 492	188-90

QUESTION	DEM	RIDDICK	RONR	AIPSC
13. How can a member delay consideration of a motion for a specific period of time?	88-89	143-44	64, 179-80	61-62
14. How long can the assembly postpone consideration of a pending question?	89-90	143-44	183-84	62
15. How is a special order created?	90, 105	131-32	182, 185-88, 352	62-63
16. What are the general limits of debate?	25-26	72-74	42-44, 385-90	65-66
17. How are the limits of debate set?	90-91	75-76, 102-03	64, 191-92, 388-91	65, 131-32
18. How can members stop debate?	92-93	44-45, 75-76	64, 197-98	67-68
19. How long can a question be laid on the table?	98-99, 169	189	75-76, 209-10, 212-13, 300-02	
20. What vote is required to adopt the subsidiary motion to *Amend*?	68-69	106, 206-07	133	57-58
21. Does "question" called from the floor require the chair to close debate?	93-94		202, 207, 385	69

CHAPTER 3
Privileged Motions

	QUESTION	DEM	RIDDICK	RONR	AIPSC
1.	Why can privileged motions always be made when a main motion is pending?	103-04	149-50	66-67	12
2.	Which privileged motions can sometimes interrupt a speaker?		150	221, 224-26, T 40-41	74-76
3.	What is meant by the term *Call for the Orders of the Day*?	104-05	8, 132	67, 219	
4.	If someone calls for the orders of the day, how can the assembly decide to set aside the agenda or to continue with the pending question?			221	
5.	What is a question of privilege affecting the assembly?	106-08	159-60	67, 224, 227	75
6.	What is a question of personal privilege?	106-08	159-60	67, 224, 227	75
7.	What can members do if they disagree with the ruling of the chair on admissibility of a question of privilege?	108	160	228	74
8.	How can the assembly take a "short break" in the meeting?	112	164-65	67, 230	76-78
9.	How does a meeting *stand at ease*?			82, 250, 466	
10.	How do members terminate a meeting?	113-14	4	68-69, 233-34	78-79
11.	What motion is used to continue a meeting at a later time?	119	5	68, 233-34	80

12.	Which privileged motions can be raised as main motions?	103	151	68, 101-02	75-76, 78-79
13.	Which privileged motions cannot be amended?	102	150-51	221, 226-27, 236, T 42	76

Comparisons

CHAPTER 4
Incidental Motions

	QUESTION	DEM	RIDDICK	RONR	AIPSC
1.	When can a point of order be raised? Are there any exceptions?	121-24	140-41	249-51	91
2.	What decisions of the chair cannot be appealed?	131-32		256, 258-59	83
3.	Under what conditions is an appeal debatable?	127	22-23	257-58	84
4.	What is the usual vote required for suspension of the rules?	132	188	261	88
5.	Can all rules be suspended?	133	188	13, 260, 263-65, 412, 620-21	86-87
6.	What are the conditions under which the bylaws can be suspended?	133	188	13	86
7.	What is meant by the "Gordian Knot" motion?				87-88
8.	How can a motion be separated into two or more parts? Does this apply only to main motions?	137	88	270-71	98-102
9.	When can a motion be divided upon demand?		88	110, 274-75	99
10.	What is the method for verifying a voice vote?	138-39	87-88	52, 280	102-04
11.	What is the method for having a vote counted?	139-40	87-88	51-52, 411	103
12.	How can an assembly take a ballot vote?	133-34	99-100	283	151
13.	What is the vote required to close nomination? Why is it higher than the vote to re-open nominations?	135	123	288-89	160-61

	QUESTION	DEM	RIDDICK	RONR	AIPSC
14.	What are the methods for making nominations?	84, 239-40	123	288, 431	159-60
15.	What is the procedure used for resigning?	205-07	110, 174	291-92, 467	265-66
16.	Does a member need permission to read from correspondence or a book while speaking in debate?	142-43	164	292-93, 298-99	129
17.	Is asking a speaker a question permitted?	125	138	294-95	94-95
18.	How can a member find out which motion to make or if something is in order?	124	138-40	293-94	93-94
19.	How is a request for an unspecified privilege handled?	146	172-73	299	96
20.	Does the motion Object to the Consideration of a Question affect members' rights?	141		268	
21.	How does the chair put the vote on an *Objection to the Consideration of a Question*?	141-42	82	269-70	

CHAPTER 5
Motions That Bring the Question Back

	QUESTION	DEM	RIDDICK	RONR	AIPSC
1.	After a motion is sent to a committee, how can the assembly resume consideration of the motion?	83-84, 171	83	310-11	43-44
2.	What happens to a standing committee when the motion is returned to the assembly?	277	48-49	313	191
3.	What happens to a special committee when a motion is returned to the assembly?	277	48	313	191
4.	What vote is needed to reconsider the vote on a main motion?	152	166	320	47
5.	When is it impossible to reconsider a main motion?	157	166	316-17, T 46-47	45
6.	Can a vote on a subsidiary motion be reconsidered?	155	166	319	45, 48
7.	What is the time limit involved in reconsidering a motion?	153, 158	166-67	316-17	48
8.	What is the motion to *Reconsider and Enter on the Minutes?"*	160-61		332-33	
9.	When can a motion to *Rescind* not be used?	166	173	308	48
10.	What motion is used to change the text of a previously adopted motion?	171	41-43	305	40-41, 58
11.	What is meant by the motion to *Rescind and Expunge?* What vote is required and how does this affect the previously approved minutes?	167-68	94-95	310, 404	

QUESTION	DEM	RIDDICK	RONR	AIPSC
12. By what process may a defeated motion be restored to consideration?	152, 172	166-67, 168-69	315, 336	24-25, 46-48
13. What vote is required to amend the bylaws?	187	37	307, 592	244

	QUESTION	DEM	RIDDICK	RONR	AIPSC
1.	What kinds of meetings are there?	13-14, 108	21, 106, 183	89-99	105-10
2.	What is an annual meeting?	291	21-22	94-95	112
3.	What is the difference between a meeting and a session?		182	81-82	
4.	Does the time between regular meetings have any procedural effect?			90-91	62, 77, 81
5.	What is an adjourned or a continued meeting?	13-14	4-5	93-94	80, 107-08
6.	What are the limits on special meetings?	13	183-84	91-93	106-07
7.	Can an item rejected at one meeting be considered at another meeting?	172	168-69	88, 336-37, 339-40	25
8.	What is an executive or closed session?	276	45-46	95-96	108-09
9.	How are the minutes of an executive session handled?		46	96	109, 228-29
10.	What is a quorum?	148	161-62	21, 345	122
11.	How is a quorum calculated?	151	162	21, 345-46	122-24
12.	What actions can be taken in the absence of a quorum?	148-49	163	347-48	122
13.	How can an action that is taken at a meeting without a quorum be made legitimate?	150	63	124-25, 348, 487	41-42, 122

QUESTION	DEM	RIDDICK	RONR	AIPSC
14. What is a "point of no quorum?"	149	162-63	349	124 (point of order)
15. What rules apply to electronic meetings?			97-99	109-10
16. May committees meet electronically?			98, 499	194

Comparisons

CHAPTER 7
Order of Business and Debate

	QUESTION	DEM	RIDDICK	RONR	AIPSC
1.	What is the standard order of business?	14, 18-19	130-31	353	115
2.	What is an agenda and how does it become effective?		7	371, 372	116-17
3.	What is a consent agenda or a consent calendar?		56	361	120-21, 220-21
4.	Is there a difference between an agenda and a program?	15	7	27, 351-53, 352n, 373	116, 209-10
5.	How can members change the order of business?	132, 170-71	7, 130-31	363-64	116
6.	How can the assembly take up something that is scheduled later in the order of business?	132	7-8, 130-31	373	116
7.	Can a member give his right to debate to another member?			388	132
8.	What is considered improper debate?	31	72-74	391-94	130
9.	How can a non-member enter into debate?			263n	85-86
10.	Under what circumstances can the presiding officer enter into debate?	41-43, 128-29	23, 74	394-95	83, 131, 176, 190
11.	What actions can be taken when a member enters into improper debate?	31-32	84	450, 645-46	130
12.	What are the rules for assigning the floor?	43-44	72	378-83	127-28

CHAPTER 8
Voting

QUESTION	DEM	RIDDICK	RONR	AIPSC
1. How is a majority determined?	36	106	400	135
2. When is the president entitled to vote?	45	146	405-06	142-43
3. May honorary members vote?	304	100, 198	463	181
4. What is a two-thirds vote?	36	207	401	22-23, 143, 149, 308
5. What is meant by a vote of a majority of the membership?	151	106	403	138
6. What is a plurality voting?	246	140	404-05	140-41
7. What is meant by a cumulative vote?		200	443-44	275
8. What is a straw vote?			429	158
9. What is the function of proxy voting?	33	155-56	428-29	153-55, 285-86, 306
10. What are the methods of voting?	32-33	197-205	409-10	147-58
11. How can someone be elected who was not nominated?	209, 247	205	431	161
12. How are the results of a voice vote verified?	138	87-88	280	103
13. Are illegal votes counted in determining a majority?	246, 248	197-98	416	168, 287
14. May ex officio members vote?	274	94	483	190
15. Can a member abstain?	37	2	45, 407	140
16. When can a member change his or her vote?	37-38	111	48, 408, 421	157
17. What is preferential voting?		145	425-28	156-57
18. What is ballot voting?	32, 244-45, 309	198-99	412	151

19. How is a roll call vote conducted?	38	202-03	420-22	150-51
20. How can an election be conducted when there is only one nominee for an office?	245, 248	3	443, 573	168-69
21. When should a mail ballot be used?	33	103-04	424	152
22. Is a vote valid if the motion is not seconded?	53		36-37	20
23. What is bullet voting?	247	199	407	275
24. What is absentee voting?	33	1-2, 198	423-24	152-55
25. What are voting cards?			411-12	150
26. What is electronic voting?		199	419	153
27. What is a signed ballot?		200	420	150-51
28. How long should ballots be kept?	213, 249-50	192	418-19	
29. What is the principle of one person-one vote?	243		407	275

Comparisons 49

CHAPTER 9
Officers and Documents of Authority

	QUESTION	DEM	RIDDICK	RONR	AIPSC
1.	What defines the offices and the duties of the officers of an organization?	179, 250-58	124-25	447, 572-73	181-83
2.	What is the minimum number of officers necessary for conducting business?		109	22	178
3.	What are the procedural duties of the presiding officer?	250-52	146	449-50	174-76
4.	How are vacancies filled? What about vacancies in the office of president?	180, 255	127, 196-97	457, 458, 467-68, 575	177, 184-85
5.	Who presides if the president and vice president are absent from the meeting?	40, 252	147-48	452-54	176-77
6.	Does the president have the power to appoint committees?	83-84	50-51	456, 495-96, 579, 587, 640-41	181-82
7.	How should the presiding officer be referred to by the members and by himself?	27, 40, 251	72	22-24, 458	27
8.	What items go into the minutes?	23-24	114-16	468-71	229-30
9.	How are minutes approved when there is only one meeting per year?	23	21-22	94-95, 474-75	232-33
10.	Minutes have been approved and later an error is discovered. How may the minutes be corrected?	21, 109, 170	114	475	232

11.	Members cannot agree on the corrections to the minutes being approved. What do we do?	22	114	354-55	117, 231
12.	A member wants to "dispense with the minutes." What does that mean?	22-23, 170, 224		474	234-35
13.	How is the treasurer's report verified?	253	25-26	479-80, 627	249-50
14.	If the society has a separate constitution and bylaws, which is superior to the other?	178	89	14	238
15.	Does custom supersede the rules in a parliamentary manual?	243-44	70	19	3, 245
16.	What is the vote needed for a society to adopt parliamentary rules that differ from the parliamentary authority?	181	184	17, 122	245
17.	Can a rule in the bylaws be suspended?	133	188	13, 17, 88, 260-63	86
18.	What normally should be included in the bylaws?	178-79	34-36	13, 570-83	239, 299-301
19.	When do the rules in the parliamentary authority not apply?	179, 312	179	16	5, 245, 272

CHAPTER 10
Boards and Committees

	QUESTION	DEM	RIDDICK	RONR	AIPSC
1.	Do all organizations have a board of directors?	270	27	482	195
2.	Are officers automatically on the board of directors?	270	28	451-62, 482	195
3.	How is board procedure different from regular meeting procedure?	273	28-29	487-88	273
4.	Can boards adopt their own rules?	270-71	28	486	195
5.	I'm a member of the organization but not of the board. Can I attend board meetings?		28	95-96	108
6.	How is an executive committee created?	179, 269, 270	93	485, 577, 582-83	196
7.	How are standing committees created?	277	48-49	490-92	188
8.	How are special committees created?	82-84, 87, 274-75	48-50	171-72, 492-97, 579, 587	188-89
9.	What happens to an unfinished assignment to a special committee when a new administration is elected?	277	53	502-03	188, 191
10.	Can people who are members of the organization, but not on the committee, attend committee meetings?	275-76	53	95-96, 501	108, 192
11.	What is done at a committee hearing?	289-90	99	501, 637-38	194, 214-17
12.	Can the chairman of a committee participate in debate in a committee meeting?	275	52	488, 500	189

13. Can committees appoint sub-committees?	277	53	497	192
14. Are minority reports from committees automatically presented to the assembly?	283	112-13	527-28	203
15. What can the assembly do if a committee doesn't report?	83-84	83	310-13	43-44, 191
16. What rules govern the reconsideration of a vote in a committee?	273	166-67	315, 329-30	44-48, 193-94

CHAPTER 11
Disciplinary Actions

QUESTION		DEM	RIDDICK	RONR	AIPSC
1.	How is an assembly protected from annoyance by nonmembers in a meeting?	109		644-45, 648-49	8, 108, 181
2.	How does the chair deal with minor breaches of order by a member?	31, 40-41	83-85	645-46	130
3.	What is "naming" a member?		84	646-48	
4.	What are the rights of a member who is subjected to disciplinary procedures?	267	193	655-56	264-65
5.	How are offences that occur outside a meeting handled?	266-69	193-94	649-50	264
6.	Why shouldn't disciplinary actions take place in open session?		194	655	108, 264
7.	Who can represent the accused in a trial?	268	195	664	264
8.	How are officers removed under disciplinary procedures?	266-69	86, 193-94	651-54	186
9.	What is a motion of censure and what effect does it have?	260-61	40	643	
10.	What is a vote of no confidence and what effect does it have?	259-60			
11.	What is "putting a motion from the member's place?"		85	650-51, 652n	
12.	What are the grounds for expelling a member?	266-67	84	645-48, 649-50	263-64

CHAPTER 12
What is the Difference in the Terms

TERMS	DEM	RIDDICK	RONR	AIPSC
1. Constitution – Bylaws	177-78	31, 58	12-14, 565	238-39
2. Merger – Consolidation		57, 111-12	561	
3. Precedence – Precedent	12	117, 144	60n, 60-61, 251-52	23, 306
4. Bylaws – Standing Rules	177, 181	31, 184	12, 18, 565	239, 245
5. Order of Business – Agenda	14, 18-19	7, 130-31	25-27, 351-53, 371	115-17
6. Executive Board – Executive Committee	197, 269-70	27-28, 93-94	481-83, 485	195-96
7. Executive Board – Executive Session	269-70, 276	27, 45-46	95-96, 481-83	108, 195-96, 303
8. Candidate – Nominee	239	39	430-31	160-61
9. Consensus – General/Unanimous Consent	309	56, 97, 194-95	54-55	148
10. Recess – Adjourn - Stand At Ease	112, 113	4, 164-65,	67-68, 82-85, 230-42, 250, 466	76-79
11. Reconsider – Rescind	152, 165	165-66, 173-74	305, 315	44-49
12. Meeting – Session	13, 202	108, 182	2, 81-84, 94	105
13. Privileged Motion – Question of Privilege	102, 106, 110	150, 159	66-67, 224-25	73

Comparisons

45775989R00039

Made in the USA
Middletown, DE
13 July 2017